WHAT THEY
HAVE
TAUGHT ME

WHAT THEY HAVE TAUGHT ME

Encouragement and Hope from an Elementary School Classroom

Daniel John Fiore, Jr.

ISBN 13: 978-0-615-96206-1
ISBN 10: 0615962068
Library of Congress Catalog Card Number: 2009906235

DEDICATION

To my Heavenly Father for His constant source of love, mercy, blessing, and guidance in my life demonstrated through His son Jesus and His Holy Spirit.

To my entire family, especially my mom, dad and brother, Brian, who have always been there to offer their love and support. To my best friend, Paul, for his encouragement, prayers and spiritual support especially throughout this project.

To all my students who have taught me lessons about life and faith in their own special and unique ways. These spiritual lessons are helping to make me into who God wants me to be. To express my gratitude, a portion of the proceeds from the sale of this book will be used to help establish student scholarships.

CONTENTS

INTRODUCTION

Mr. Fiore's Class Schedule:
8:00 AM – 9:00 AM – Reading
9:00 AM – 10:00 AM – Writing
10:00 AM – 11:00 AM – Math
11:00 AM – 1:00 PM – Lunch/Recess
1:00 PM – 1:30 PM – Science
1:30 PM – 2:00 PM – Spelling

As a child, this schedule was fastened to my brown bedroom closet door with brightly colored thumbtacks. On some days reading might be last and spelling first, but this is how I remembered it. I always made sure there was ample time for my childhood favorites: lunch and recess. As soon as I arrived home from elementary school, my bedroom was transformed into Mr. Fiore's classroom. It was complete with a small chalkboard with colored chalk and an eraser, school textbooks, notebooks, a teacher's desk, and stuffed animals as pretend students. Occasionally, I would convince my little brother, Brian, to join my class, but that usually did not last long once he heard the word "homework."

I loved to play school growing up. I loved to be the teacher and organize the schedule and best of all write on the chalkboard. Grading imaginary papers with my own red pen was fun too. On days when I was home sick from real school I would often "spy" from the top of our stairs down into my mom's nursery school, which she operated out of our house while we were growing up. I listened intently to her and watched as the children played, colored, and created projects. I was fascinated with everything to do with school! I remember thinking it would be neat to be a real teacher someday, but never imagined that is where my life would lead me.

I always believed that the teacher would teach and the students were just there to learn—the same way it worked back in my imaginary classroom. God, however, had a different idea; He wanted *me* to learn what true knowledge was all about. Over the last several years, I have been faithfully reading the Bible, which has led to a deeper, more personal relationship with Jesus. The more I read, the more I could see how Jesus was actively helping me learn true wisdom. One particular Bible verse was continually brought to my mind: "But when the Holy Spirit controls our lives, He will produce this kind of fruit in us: love, joy, peace, patience, kindness, goodness, faithfulness, gentleness and self-control..." (Gal. 5:22-23 NLT). I never really understood how to fully develop these virtues in my life. But as I've yielded my life to Him, and with time and patience, the Holy Spirit has been developing these in my life in very personal and meaningful ways. I started out my spiritual education with many questions and have been slowly learning all the right answers.

Doubt, Fear, and Worry

"Don't worry about anything; instead, pray about everything. Tell God what you need, and thank Him for all He has done. If you do this, you will experience God's peace, which is far more wonderful than the human mind can understand. His peace will guard your hearts and minds as you live in Christ Jesus."

—Phil. 4:6-7 NLT

P ress one to accept this position or two to cancel." My fingers hovered over the telephone keypad with my mind trapped between doubt and fear. My thoughts were interrupted by the automated voice again. "Press one to accept this position or two to cancel." I quickly pressed one. "Your job number is 247712. Thank you for using Sub Search." With my heart pounding in my chest, I hung up the phone. I had no idea that within hours I would be on the phone again, pleading desperately for help.

I crept up to the front doors of the elementary school for my first substitute teaching assignment. Doubt, worry, and fear rushed through my mind. *Could I handle the students? What would happen if they didn't listen to me? Would there be lesson plans? How will I remember all their names? How will I find my way around the school?*

My jumbled thoughts were interrupted by a pleasant voice greeting me at the front office. The receptionist welcomed me and asked me to sign in. She confirmed that I would be substituting for first grade. She gave me a map of the school and I quickly studied it. I'm not good with directions so I clung tightly to the map. With trepidation, I made my way through the maze of hallways trying to find the classroom. After making several wrong turns and fearing I would walk into the wrong classroom, I finally asked another teacher for help. She smiled at me and escorted me to the correct classroom.

As I entered the classroom, I quickly put down my bag and searched for the lesson plans. I carefully read through them again and again as I watched the clock. Thank God, I had arrived early; I'd already lost twenty minutes just trying to find the classroom! It was now 7:35 AM and school began at 8:00 AM. My heart pounded and my mind raced with worry and doubt. *Why did I do this? I'm not prepared and I'm not sure how I'm going to get through the day.* After studying the lesson plans again and trying to search through the handouts and teacher editions, I tossed blank name cards on each desk.

Just then, three students flew into the room followed by at least twenty more, all laughing and talking. I heard one of the students yell, "Yeah, we have a substitute today!"

Another student asked, "Hey Mister, what's your name?"

"Mr. Fiore and I will be your teacher today," I replied. After they all arrived, I closed the door but they would not settle down. My worst fears were becoming reality. A red-headed boy in the front began jabbing himself with a pencil all over his arm. I walked over and lowered my voice, saying, "Please stop." He ignored me. I asked him again to stop but he kept it up. Meanwhile, the rest of the room was in chaos. The students were scrambling around the room and yelling back and forth. Out of the corner of my eye, I saw a bell on the teacher's desk so I darted over and began to ring it, thinking this would calm them down. Nothing happened: they just got louder. I rang the bell even harder but it could barely be heard over the clamor.

Just then I realized the Pledge of Allegiance and morning announcements were on and I tried to set the TV to Channel 3 as the lesson plans stated, but the channel would not change. I asked one of the students to help, but she ignored me. I finally found Channel 3 just as the principal was wrapping up the morning announcements. Of course, no one was listening. I went back to the bell and rang it over and over again, then said, "Boys and girls please be quiet; I need your attention." I raised my voice and said it again. *I knew I should not have done this teaching thing. What am I going to do now?*

I noticed an adjoining door to the next classroom so I opened it. I observed a very quiet and well-behaved classroom in progress. I looked at the teacher and whispered, "Excuse me, but I need a little help over here." The teacher told her students to read quietly and, just like robots, they listened. She then walked over to me.

"I can see you need some help," she said and smiled. She came into my classroom while I stood at the door and watched her students in amazement. She got up in front of my students and with a hand signal and firm voice demanded their attention. The room went silent. It was a miracle! She told the class that their behavior was unacceptable and they were disturbing *her* class. She introduced me to the class again and warned them to be on their best behavior.

She also told them that she wanted to give their teacher a great report when she returned tomorrow. I thanked the teacher profusely and began to feel a bit more in control. I wished she could have stayed with me but she returned to her classroom.

With the students now quiet I began to explain the schedule for the day. I asked them to write their name on their name card as I took attendance. Some did and some didn't. I asked them to please do as I asked, but only a few listened and I praised them for it. Next, I got the small reading group started and assigned work to the rest of the class. When I told the students they needed their crayons for the project, they jumped out of their seats and ran to their book bags and "cubbies." As the noise level jumped again my fears and worries came rushing back. *What now?* I begged them to quiet down by ringing the bell. I tried to remember the hand signal the other teacher used. Some responded but most just kept talking and moving around the room. I finally raised my voice. "If you all do not quiet down and get back to your seats I'm going to call the office!" I paused and watched one student return to her seat while the others ignored me. "I mean it!" I then grabbed the phone and called the office. They could barely hear me on the other end.

"Can you *please* send someone to help me? I cannot get these students to quiet down and listen to me." I went back to the front of the room and tried again to gain control. I watched two girls arguing over a pack of crayons. I tried to intervene, but they completely ignored me. Finally one of the girls started crying. I begged the girl to stop but she continued even louder. Fear and worry crippled me and I could only wait for help.

Suddenly the classroom door flew open and the assistant principal stormed into the classroom. The class froze. I explained the problem to him. He ordered the students back to their seats immediately without making a sound. They quickly obeyed. He then told them he was staying in the room, while I went ahead with my teaching. Relief and pressure coursed through me at the same time. I also felt embarrassed because the assistant principal had to "rescue me." I tried to gather my thoughts and went back to the lesson plans. After instructing the class I started the small reading groups once again. The assistant principal remained in the back of the room.

By lunchtime I was relieved to have a break. The students lined up, then left the room, along with the assistant principal. I thanked him again and apologized for taking up so much of his day.

After lunch I went to the cafeteria to pick up the students. I tried counting them to make sure I had everyone. We went outside for recess. As soon as the students saw the playground, they bolted.

"Slow down, please, slow down!" I said in vain. I saw several other teachers outside talking and began worrying that they were talking about me. However, I soon found out they were sympathetic and told me they understood how difficult the first day of teaching can be, especially as a substitute.

We started to have a great conversation when one of the students ran up to me yelling, "Two boys are trying to escape under the fence!" I raced through the sand in my new black dress shoes and yelled at the students to stop. They just kept digging and there was a pretty big hole under the fence. Another teacher followed behind me and took the boys by the hand to the concrete sidewalk.

"Stand here and take a timeout," she told them firmly. I stood there shocked, amazed, and embarrassed as I emptied the sand out my shoes. I checked around to try to account for my other students, but all I saw was a sea of blue shirts and khaki pants. I asked the other teacher, "How will I know which students are mine?"

She just laughed and said, "We will help you." They helped me gather all the students and then we headed inside. Of course, I needed help finding my way back to the classroom and the line leader reminded me which way we needed to go. As we walked back, the assistant principal passed us and asked how things were going. "Okay," I said.

When we got back to class I noticed several of the students were covered in sand and had dirt marks on their clothes. I let them get water and noticed it was only 1:00 PM. *I still have one hour to go! What do I do now? What happens if they start to act up again?* Fear gripped me. I grabbed the chapter book their teacher had been reading from her desk and started reading aloud. Some put their heads down and others just listened. I could not believe it. I actually had control over the class! I began to feel a sense of confidence but it was quickly shattered as some boys began throwing paper balls at some girls in the back of the room.

I walked back toward them while reading and grabbed the paper from them. Somehow, I made it through to 1:50 and the end of the day! Relieved, I told the students to pack up and of course they started talking and getting up out of their seats. I tried in vain to settle them down. Finally the bell rang and this time it worked. They all scurried out of the room. Peace reigned as I sat back in the teacher's chair, filled with relief. As I wrote a note for the teacher, I realized I had not accomplished half of what she had left in the lesson plans. I felt like a failure. I packed up my bag and headed to the office to check out, thinking I'll never be back. Teaching was not for me.

As I lay in bed that night, I relived the events of the day and thought about what I could have done differently. I had been praying for months for direction on a career path since I felt I needed a change. I remember asking God, "Why did nothing go right today? Should I just stay in my current job as regional director of sales and forget this prompting to try teaching? Was that what you were trying to show me today?"

The next day I couldn't stop thinking about the students and what had happened. I felt an urge to call the teacher of the class and offer her an explanation. I called the school for her number, then dialed it. I explained what happened and apologized. She was very understanding.

As I was talking, an idea popped into my mind to go back to the class and "job shadow" her for the day to see how she handled the students. She agreed. After getting permission from the school administration, I asked for another personal day from work, then we set a date. I was amazed watching her handle the class. The same rambunctious students I tried to control were well-behaved and listened attentively. I observed how the mistakes I made could have been avoided. I learned volumes that day from the students and how best to reach them. I even spent one-on-one time with several and got to know them better.

To my surprise, the girl who was crying over the pack of crayons had lost her grandmother that week, her only guardian, and she was placed into a foster home. I realized she wasn't crying over the crayons. The red-headed boy who had jabbed himself with the pencils had several self-destructive tendencies and emotional issues. He was really a very sweet child who just needed attention and emotional support. Another boy who was reluctant to read during reading group had been teased by some other students because of his reading difficulties. He hated to read out loud and would often avoid it by being disruptive. My eyes were opened that day in many ways; I saw so many students who just wanted attention, love, and care. A seed was planted in my heart that day.

The days passed and I continued in my current corporate job while looking for full-time teaching work. I believe God was showing me that a teaching career was His plan for me, but I just had to trust Him. I had to put my worries, fears, and doubts aside. I substituted a few more times at several others schools. I had interesting experiences, but nothing as compared to my first time. I continued to pray and trust that God would bring me to the right opportunity. I was turned down for several teaching positions because of my lack of experience, and again began to doubt if this was really for me.

God kept watering that seed in my heart through the support of my best friend who believed this was my calling. He encouraged me daily and would remind me of Bible passages like Philippians 4:6-7, which I listed at the beginning of this chapter. It served as a constant source of hope.

As the summer passed, I again began to worry and doubt if I was ever going to get a teaching job. It is amazing how worry and doubt can make you question yourself and your instincts. A few days later, I received a call from a principal I had interviewed with at a career fair. He offered me a fifth grade teaching position at an excellent school. I was so excited and finally began to feel things falling into place! I scheduled a meeting with him to fill out my new hire paperwork. As soon as I got off the phone, I started worrying about how I was going to handle a classroom of fifth graders. I could barely handle first graders! I tried not to let my anxious feelings overwhelm the excitement of the moment.

I went to sleep that night assured that I was about to begin a new chapter in my life and that my prayers had been answered. That all changed the following day when I received a call from the assistant principal at that same school telling me that the position they offered me was no longer available because one of their teachers decided not to retire. I was shocked and disappointed. My first thought, once again, was to question my calling to be a teacher. My mind raced with questions and doubts about my next steps. Over the next few days I slowly started to reconcile myself to the fact that maybe God's will was for me to stay in the corporate world.

August rolled around and I still had no job offers. I kept reminding myself that God's plan and timing is always perfect. I continued praying and trusting and hoping for direction. Ironically, I received a call from a teacher at one of the schools I had substituted at earlier in the year; she wanted me to substitute for her again. We started talking and she told me there was a full-time opening for a fifth grade teacher, and asked me to drop off my resume.

A glimpse of excitement and hope sparked on the inside of me. It was one of the top 100 schools in the state of Florida. I loved the school, the staff, and the atmosphere when I substituted there. Then my excitement and hope suddenly gave way to doubt; I began to doubt I even had a chance. They rarely had teaching positions available and most likely someone else with more experience would be chosen. I felt it was going to be impossible, but I would later learn that anything is possible with God if you surrender to His perfect will and timing.

A few days after the interview, I did not hear anything so I called the school and was informed by the principal's assistant that I was not the right fit for the fifth grade job. My heart sank. I was disappointed to say the least. As I held the phone in my hand and once again entertained the thought that teaching must not be for me, my thoughts were interrupted by an offer to come and interview for a third grade position instead. Disappointment immediately turned into excitement and I grabbed the opportunity.

Days later, after riding this emotional roller coaster, I interviewed yet once again. This time it was with the entire third grade team of teachers. I was nervous and feared that I was not impressing any of them. I finished the interview after answering all their questions and asking some of my own. I wasn't sure what to think. I thanked each of them and walked out of the school. All of a sudden I heard one of the teachers call to me to come back to the office for a minute. I thought maybe I forgot something. As I walked into the office, they all yelled "Congratulations!" The principal along with the team of teachers officially offered me the position to teach third grade. I could not believe it! It was a moment I will never forget. The war of worry and doubt ended and I felt encouraged and validated. All the disappointments and struggles I experienced leading up to this day made me appreciate the magnitude of the moment even more. Despite what I was feeling, I was reminded I needed to keep my faith and trust God's perfect plan and timing. Faith should not be moved by feelings. That was easier said now that the situation was over. God once again proved faithful as He had done countless times before in my life.

I had only three days to prepare for the first day of school with my very own class. I had no idea that being a teacher was going to impact my life in so many ways. I thought I would be the one teaching the students everything they needed to know, the same way it worked back in my imaginary classroom as a child. But God had a different idea about what true knowledge was all about. The plan was to use my students to teach me.

LESSON LEARNED: Fear, doubt, and worry produce nothing. Fear and doubt can keep us from our destiny and worry can alter our purpose. I'm learning to trust God in all things by surrendering my heart and mind to His will like Jesus did. I'm learning that faith should not be contingent on how I feel. I'm learning that life may not unfold exactly as I expect, but it will be exactly what I need.

PATIENCE AND SELF-CONTROL

"Knowing God leads to self-control. Self-control leads to patient endurance, and patient endurance leads to godliness."

—2 Pet. 1:6 NLT

I entered Room 114 knowing I had only three days to prepare myself and my new classroom for my first class. I stared around at the bare white walls and the empty desks. There were tons of books piled on the counter near the window and a banner on one wall that stated "Vocabulary Rodeo" and featured a lasso surrounding some words. I did not know where to begin.

My frantic thoughts were interrupted by a friendly voice that asked, "Do you need some help?

I hope you don't mind, but I started setting up the room for you." I immediately felt a sense of relief. God provided me the help and support He knew I would need in the form of a mentor. She was a fellow third grade teacher who stood by my side and helped me with all the details. Over the next several days she also provided me with something I had not been thinking too much about with everything going on—self-confidence. Believe it or not the classroom was ready for the "big day" thanks to her help. I, on the other hand, was not. I still had lesson plans to write and wasn't sure how to do them. I had teacher editions to review, orientation packets to prepare, class lists to review and so much more.

Despite my fears and worries about encountering another group of students, everything went well the first day. Once again, I received reaffirmation about the deceptive nature of fear and worry. I quickly got into a routine and began to learn what techniques and strategies worked and which ones didn't.

As I got to know each of my twenty-eight third graders, the learning really began. I remember asking Pedro, a shy and dark-haired boy who sat in the front row, a question about one of the vocabulary words we learned. He did not respond. I asked him again and still no response. I began to panic and walked over to him to make sure he was okay. I then heard him whisper, "No habla Ingles." Luckily, I knew some Spanish and realized he was saying he did not speak English. *How am I going to be able to teach this student if he doesn't understand English? What do I do with him?* After a brief writing assignment, I also discovered he could not even write a word in English either. I tried to communicate with him, but it was useless. Luckily, another student who was bi-lingual offered to help by translating for him. This seemed to be a temporary solution to the problem.

As the weeks passed, I found myself becoming edgy with him. He needed so much one-on-one assistance that it was almost impossible for me to get anything else done. I'm someone who likes order and structure and I don't have much patience when my plans go unaccomplished. On top of that, I was still learning how best to teach certain concepts to the class, how to best manage my time and how to maintain order and control. I was also learning how to have self-control over my emotions and my words to make sure I did not say anything that might make him feel badly, even though he probably would not have understood me.

There were many times, however, when I was tempted to vent my frustration on him. I was forced to become the student and research various programs that I could implement independently to better assist him with learning English. It was overwhelming at times, but I managed to get through it. I was able to find several internet-based programs that were able to assist him with building his vocabulary. He worked hard on these programs and was willing to do anything to be able to speak English like everyone else. I will never forget the first time he read a sentence out loud in English. The entire class burst out loud in cheers and clapping. His enormous smile was priceless. Pedro taught me a valuable lesson that day; he taught me that being a teacher requires much patience, but with patience comes progress, and with progress comes pride. He showed me that it was more important for each student to grasp what was being taught then it was for me to feel I accomplished every detail in my daily lesson. He reminded me that I need to guard my tongue by practicing self-control, especially in stressful times, so I that I would avoid saying something that could discourage a child's progress.

My first year continued to fly by and I was learning more and more each day from my students, my peers and from myself about what it takes to be a successful teacher. I was getting into a groove and things were flowing rather smoothly until I received a call from the principal telling me that a new student was being assigned to my class and he was going to start tomorrow. At first I did not think anything of it until I heard about some of the challenges other teachers had with this particular student. *Why do I have to deal with this? When things were finally going smoothly and I began to feel more confident in my skills and abilities.* I would soon learn once again that God always has a reason for the trials and difficulties He sends into our lives. I spent most of that night worrying and fearing the worst even though I had learned just how unproductive those emotions can be.

Morning arrived quickly and I began my thirty minute commute to school. I remember praying for patience in my car so I would not jump to conclusions about how things in my classroom might change and for self-control to help me avoid saying what I truly felt about this situation. After meeting the student I soon realized that my patience would be tested once again. As I walked over to greet him I noticed he was pretty tall for a third grader. I later learned that he was retained in the past and really should have been in fourth grade. He had a very difficult time following directions and completing his work. He was easily distracted and had a hard time staying focused on anything. This pattern of behavior continued constantly over the next several weeks. I tried everything to keep him focused. I had several talks with him, moved him to the front of the room, researched behavior strategies, spoke with other teachers, tried incentives and rewards, spoke to his father, but nothing seemed to work. It was especially frustrating to me because he was capable and bright. He had potential, but was not making any effort. There were so many days that year that I lost my patience and did not have self-control over my emotions. I would often ask him, "Why can't you just complete these assignments? Why can't you just finish your homework? Why can't you pay attention and listen when I'm trying to help you?" My questions would go unanswered.

My first year was coming to a close and I was still not seeing much change in his behavior. He did put forth a bit more effort when coerced by me, but when asked to complete work independently usually little was accomplished. I often went home feeling like a failure and wondering what else I could have done to help reach this student and motivate him.

On the last day of school I handed each student a card I had made especially for them. I noticed his eyes began to fill with tears. Once he saw me looking at him he changed his expression and acted as if he had something stuck in his eye. I realized that maybe I did reach him that year. I still had doubts though. As I look back now, I believe he taught me that, although on the outside things may not appear to be changing, on the inside seeds of hope are being planted. I believe God used him to teach me it is not always about seeing immediate results, but believing the results are possible if you are patient and willing to surrender your efforts and hopes to His perfect care. I know this was a lesson in self-control and I discovered I had much more to learn. I needed to practice controlling my emotions, something that doesn't come easy to me. I needed to learn to remain calm and to set a better example for my students on how best to act (not react) when upset.

Over the years as a teacher, I have learned daily lessons on practicing patience and self-control. These are just two examples of impactful lessons I have learned and not forgotten. By nature I am emotional, not patient. I want things done when I want them done. I expect my students to listen to directions the first time they are given. It frustrates me when I have to repeat myself over and over. I'm very detail-oriented and focused on accomplishing my goals. I often lose my patience when things don't work out the way I planned or in the timeframe I allotted. It is often a challenge to exercise self-control when I'm upset. I'm sometimes ready to say exactly what I feel when I know I should not let my emotions get the best of me.

Being a teacher has really challenged me to change in this area more so than any other area in my life and it is a continual process. I believe God is using my classroom experiences to remind me just how patient He has been with me through my learning process. Each and every day, I struggle with and pray for patience and self-control; patience to listen to my students and self-control; so that I'm not tempted to do all the talking; patience to make sure they understand the lesson before moving onto the next one and self-control to make sure I do not speak discouraging words to them when I feel frustrated; patience to explain directions for a project or assignment in different ways using different strategies and self-control to know that sometimes I may need to repeat myself calmly to ensure they understand it; patience to deal with student arguments and disagreements that I may feel are trivial and self-control to help me avoid saying something that might make them feel I don't care; patience to understand that I may not reach or motivate every student to the degree I would like and the self-control to know that I will never stop trying; patience to let go and let God work through me and through my students and self-control to not let my feelings affect my faith.

LESSON LEARNED: Patience and self-control do not come naturally and mastering them is a lifelong process. I'm learning to allow God to use the people and circumstances in my life to slowly change me into who He wants me to be. It has been painful at times, but powerful!

GOD'S GOODNESS

"God has given gifts to each of you from His great variety of spiritual gifts. Manage them well so that God's generosity can flow through you."

—1 Pet. 4:10 NLT

NNOCENT!" That was the verdict from the jury of twelve third graders. Dressed in a black gown with gavel in my hand (really just a hammer) I declared from my front desk, "Case closed!" Both the defendant and the plaintiff, along with their lawyers and witnesses, were free to go back to their seats. Class could resume again now that the defendant was found innocent of throwing food at the plaintiff in the cafeteria. The bailiff and the court reporter helped return the courtroom back to a classroom.

As a child I discovered creativity by using my imagination, but as an adult I have found it much harder to express creativity. I often have a hard time coming up with creative solutions to challenges and problems in the classroom. That was until I met this very creative and unique student. Even her name was unique and one I had never heard.

Iolani had a natural gift to be able to write and draw in ways that really amazed me and others around her. She wrote and illustrated stories with creative plots and characters. I still have one of the books that she produced through our school's student publishing program. I read it aloud every year to each of my classes and it is always a favorite.

I would ask her how she came up with such interesting ideas and she would state very frankly, "Well, the ideas just pop into my head." Several times that first year I had issues with students arguing and teasing other students. Unfortunately, this happened most of the time at lunch or recess when I was not directly involved. I would do my best to be the mediator and let each student state his or her case, but often it was difficult to know who was at fault. Once she introduced me to a concept she called "Class Court" things began to take a dramatic turn in the classroom.

She explained that she had this idea based on court shows she watched on television. The students with the issues could be the plaintiff and the defendant and they would state their case to the rest of the class which would be the "jury."

"Mr. Fiore, you can be the judge to help solve the case," she said. I was astounded that an eight-year-old could think up such a creative and innovative idea.

I immediately thought through how this would work in the classroom setting and decided to incorporate it into one of our social studies lessons on governments and courts. The student that was accusing the other student of teasing or doing something wrong played the plaintiff. The student being accused played the defendant. The plaintiff and the defendant each were able to choose two students to represent them as their lawyers. Most of the time they chose their friends, but that was okay. If there were any witnesses who saw the event unfold they would take the appropriate sides.

We chose a student to play the role of bailiff and one to play the role of court reporter. In our social studies lesson I made sure that each of these roles were explained so the students understood them. I also had the students make vocabulary flashcards to help learn and practice these new words. The remaining students were members of the jury. It was often more than twelve, but I explained there are usually only twelve jurors in a real courtroom.

The plaintiff sat on one side with their lawyers and witnesses and the defendant sat on the other side with their lawyers and witnesses. The court reporter and bailiff stood on either side of me. The witness stand was a chair located next to me. A green vocabulary book served as the Bible where they would swear to tell the whole truth. I explained that we shouldn't use the real Bible since this was for play. The jury sat off to my left complete with one student as lead juror. I would have to help guide the course of events starting with hearing the opening comments from both sides, and then proceeding to the plaintiff stating his or her case. After doing this a few times, the students grasped the roles and flow of events.

It was a learning experience the first few times and certainly did not flow perfectly, but the students and I really got excited about the idea. I was shocked at how quickly they adapted to the roles. I had a parent volunteer in the classroom the day we had the case involving the throwing of food in the cafeteria and she could not believe these were third graders acting as lawyers, bailiffs, plaintiffs, and defendants. She did not even think third graders knew what those words meant!

My students got into the concept so much that all of a sudden they were fabricating reasons to implement "Class Court." I had to remind them that it would only be used as a last resort when we could not resolve conflicts between the involved students. Of course, it did not always work out perfectly but the effort was always worth it. To this day I have implemented "Class Court" each year and it has been remarkable to see how the students begin to take more responsibility for their behavior and accept the consequences from their actions. It also perfectly complements our third grade social studies curriculum.

Many other students along the way have taught me how to be a more creative teacher by using their talents and gifts. I recall one of my most athletic boys who offered an idea for a brain break. He asked if he could bring in a small basketball hoop and basketball and attach it to the back of the door. His idea was that at least once a day we would stop class for five minutes to shoot baskets. I told him that sounded like fun, but might interfere with our learning. Without hesitation he said, "How about you ask us a question about what we are learning and if we get the question right, we get to shoot a basket?" I loved the idea.

The next day we set up the "Slam Dunk" hoop and it was an immediate hit with all the students. Once a day we would take just five minutes and I would randomly ask two or three questions about what I was teaching. The students who got the answer correct got a chance to shoot a basket. It really helped keep the students engaged; especially those who were more likely to lose focus. The idea so inspired me that during our school's Red Ribbon Drug Free Week, I thought up the slogan, *Slam Dunk, Drugs are Junk*, which was added to the backboard of the basketball hoop. Each time a student made a basket the rest of the class would recite the slogan with them. We continued this practice for the rest of the year. I began to feel my creative side emerging. It was a small step in the right direction. Each year I have continued this idea and my students love it. It really seems to help reinforce academic skills taught in class in a fun and creative way that does not take up much time. In fact, two years later, I received a letter from one of my students stating, "Mr. Fiore, I will always remember to never do drugs because of that saying." That alone made it all worthwhile.

Through the inspiration of many of my students I gained more confidence in my own creative skills. I began researching, thinking about, and constructing projects and programs that I could use in class to help motivate and educate my students in creative ways. During an online reading workshop for teachers, I was introduced to the concept of "Reader's Theatre." Students read a script and "act out" the characters by reading with expression. I immediately implemented a "Reader's Theatre" program after having the class search the internet for student scripts. We printed and assembled them in a standing file. Students would read from various plays during small reading group after I modeled it several times for them. It helped improve their fluency and reading skills while providing them with a creative outlet and encouraged them to read with expression. It continues to be a popular reading activity in my classroom each year. I have seen great improvement in the reading scores of many of my students especially those who were reluctant to read aloud.

I also worked with fellow teachers to coordinate a program called "Writing Buddies" where students work together and become mentors for other students in writing. They enjoy working in partners and sharing ideas about the writing process. Many of the students responded positively to this activity, since it empowered them to take more responsibility for their writing and encouraged them to express their individual styles. They often felt more comfortable working on their writing one-on-one versus sharing their work in a whole group format.

My creativity continued to grow as I devised a classroom rewards program entitled "Behavior Bucks" after one of my students mentioned how fun it would be to get paid just like adults do for working hard. The program provides opportunities to reward my students for excellent behavior along with teaching them basic economic principles. I created small tickets that look like dollars and bought a storage system complete with mini drawers that serve as our "Behavior Bucks Bank." Students cannot ask for Behavior Bucks; I reward them throughout the week for excellent behavior or for completing tasks and assignments as directed. If they break a classroom rule, then they owe me a Behavior Buck for every instance. In the beginning of the year we set a class goal of how many Behavior Bucks they predict they can earn by the end of the school year. This encourages them to work together and to realize that when they earn a Behavior Buck it helps the entire class reach its goal.

Once they earn the Behavior Bucks the students deposit them into their banks until Friday. On Fridays, students count their Behavior Bucks as an extension to our math lesson. After calculating their individual weekly total, they add their balance from the previous week using a balance sheet I created.

Once they reach a pre-determined goal, they pick a small prize from "Oscar's Prize Can." The prize can, which I created from a tall white kitchen garbage can, contains a flip-up lid featuring Oscar from Sesame Street. (As a kid, I always loved watching him pop out of his can on that TV show!) The prize can is full of items like pencils, flashcards, books, and small toys. We use their individual weekly totals, which are written on the board, to calculate the class total for the week. Each Friday we add to the total to arrive at a new year-to-date grand total. The students enjoy figuring out how many more Behavior Bucks they need to reach our yearly goal. I also incorporate other math activities with the numbers from the board such as finding the median and mode or putting them in order from least to greatest. I know many teachers have similar reward systems or even more elaborate versions of this one but "Behavior Bucks" are special to me because a student inspired me to create them.

Now that my creativity was thriving, I began thinking of a way to reconnect myself and my students after they had left my classroom. I always wondered how they were doing in fourth grade and how they were changing. Of course, I would see some of them on occasion throughout the school, but we often never had time to talk. Some of them would come back and visit me after school, but most of them were busy with their new life.

One day the idea of hosting a "Reunion Breakfast" came to me. I thought it would be neat to organize a mini breakfast toward the end of each year. I would invite my students from the previous year to come, reunite and share memories. After getting approval from my principal, I made simple but festive invitations and distributed them to my former students. It was interesting to see their reactions. Many of them did not even know what a reunion was so it provided an instant opportunity to teach them a new vocabulary word.

On the morning of each Reunion Breakfast I quickly decorate the classroom with balloons, spread out some breakfast treats and place a sign on the door that says, "Welcome Back." I also take some time the week before to put photos of the students during their year with me in an album. It's been a hit with all who attend. I get to catch up with them and we reminisce about our time together. I have continued the tradition and now each class that leaves looks forward to returning for "Mr. Fiore's Reunion Breakfast." The time and effort involved in planning the reunion is small compared to the satisfaction I receive from seeing how my former students have grown and changed.

My students continually inspire me and they never cease to amaze me with their plethora of skills and talents. Some have written beautiful poems and stories. Others have drawn amazing pictures that jump off the page with vibrancy, color, and meaning. A few have mastered multiplication facts and math problems with minimal help from me. Others have sung, danced, or juggled their way through class talent shows. Still others have shown me educational programs on the computer that I did not know even existed.

Each time I witness one of my students creatively demonstrating a skill or talent I feel an urge to encourage and validate them. Once you recognize these skills and talents are given through the goodness of God it is hard not to acknowledge them.

Many of my students, like the ones I have mentioned in this chapter, have challenged me to rediscover skills and talents that I forgot I had. They have taught me that it is okay to take some risks and to bring different approaches to teaching. In fact, I feel the students respond best to lessons and activities that are creatively designed and that appeal to all learning styles. The excitement I feel from the students when delivering a well-crafted lesson is so gratifying. Being creative and using my personal gifts and talents is an essential part of teaching. I still have a lot to learn, but have been blessed with a good foundation so far. Children by nature tend to be creative and curious. Sometimes when we grow up we tend to lose that part of us. I'm so grateful to God for being placed in a career that surrounds me with plenty of opportunities to learn about creativity and to utilize my gifts and talents. After all, He is The Ultimate Creator and created all things perfect.

LESSON LEARNED: Through God's goodness, He gives each of us unique skills and talents in order to help and encourage others and to accomplish our purpose in life. As I have learned, sometimes we utilize these skills and talents instinctively and other times it takes others to help us discover them.

Lesson 4

FAITHFULNESS

"What is faith? It is the confident assurance that what we hope for is going to happen. It is the evidence of things we cannot yet see."

—Heb. 11:1 NLT

For confidentiality reasons, I will refer to him as Steven.

Steven was abandoned at a young age and placed in the foster care system. A family member offered to raise him and was his primary caretaker. During the short time he resided in foster care he experienced physical abuse.

Steven's file was about as thick as a stack of books. I usually try not to read too deeply into a student's file at first; I do not want to develop a preconceived idea about the child before getting to truly know him or her. In Steven's case, it really didn't matter whether I looked at his file or not; it was evident that there were major issues.

First of all, there were the behavioral and emotional issues. He had a hard time listening and was defiant. If he did not get his own way, he would throw himself on the floor and start yelling, screaming, and kicking. This was almost a daily occurrence. I would try telling the class to ignore him, which was almost impossible, but at times it did work. Other times I would have to call the administration to have him removed from class. Then there were the social issues. He had a hard time getting along with others and was physical with them. He would hit students or push them and then claim it was an accident. He could not sit in a team like the other students but remained in his desk next to me at all times. He often spent lunch up in the front office away from the other children.

Despite these issues, Steven was a very bright young boy and had a caring heart. He would sometimes bring a flower that he picked on the way to school for his former teacher. He was an excellent reader and would often be reading books above his level and comprehending them well. He was creative and liked to think up interesting plots and characters for his own stories. The problem was his work was often illegible and many times did not make any sense. He would get very upset when I tried to help him. I believe all he heard was negative criticism even though I was trying to offer helpful advice.

During instances like this I would use the "sandwich method," which is a helpful strategy I learned from our guidance counselor. I would provide him a compliment ("bread") followed by the area of concern ("meat") then close with another compliment ("bread"). Sometimes it worked and other times it did not. He was easily frustrated in math and often had a hard time staying focused during lessons. If I was able to keep him focused on the lesson for a few minutes, he was able to grasp the concept with some practice.

I was becoming extremely frustrated with him and his behavior and for the first time actually dreaded coming to work. My administration was very supportive, especially when other parents started calling with concerns about their children's safety and the interruptions in the classroom. My principal provided Steven with counseling and a listener once a week to listen to anything he wanted to say. A behavior specialist from the school district worked directly with me and his guardian on a comprehensive behavior plan. We did see some results and his behavior would improve for a few days at a time, but then we would end up back on square one. I knew in my heart God placed him in my care for a reason, but I did not believe I was accomplishing my purpose. I began to doubt my teaching abilities and my confidence level started to dwindle. I was beginning to lose hope.

Just when I thought things could not get any worse, he came into school one day with a bandage on the back of his ear. I asked him what happened and he did not respond. I asked him again and he told me that he got hit with a broom handle because of his behavior at school. My heart sank. I asked if I could see his ear to make sure he was okay. He pulled away the bandage and I could see a small chunk was missing from his ear. I looked into his eyes and remember seeing a deep sorrow. It is often said that "the eyes are the windows to the soul" and I believe I saw into his soul that day. I saw a lost, hurt, lonely, and scared young soul. I saw a soul who desperately needed hope. I teared up and just kept repeating over and over, "I'm so sorry this happened; I'm so sorry for everything that has happened to you."

My emotions immediately turned to anger. I wanted to call his guardian, but then those lessons on self-control reminded me to stop and think. I started thinking this was my fault. I thought if I could have just handled Steven's behavior

problems myself this may have never happened.
I could only imagine how many other times he
was punished in prior weeks. I knew he had been
abused years ago, but I never thought it could be
happening again.

After reporting everything to the administration
and filling out all the proper documentation I left for
the day. I prayed for him all night. In fact, I had been
praying all along for God to give me the wisdom,
knowledge, and strength to know how to handle him
daily. I knew I had to have faith and hope, but it was
becoming harder and harder. I remember asking God
countless times, "Father, what am I supposed to do?"

Over a week passed when I received a phone
call from our guidance counselor telling me to send
Steven to the office. He was being withdrawn from
school and was moving out of town. They did not
want him to know anything. I was shocked. Every
possible emotion ran through me. I didn't know
what to say to him. I had a student walk him to the
office and I just told him he was leaving early today.
As he left the room, my eyes remained glued on him
as he walked out the door. I knew that would be the
last I would see of him.

Later that night I called Steven's guardian and she
informed me that she was sending him back to foster
care because she could not handle him anymore. I
asked if he knew and she said, "Yes." She was in the

middle of packing his things and preparing to leave the house so I quickly asked to speak to him. She put him on the phone and all I heard was silence. I told him that I would miss him and that I'm sorry he had to leave. I said it again, "I'm sorry." His guardian snatched the phone from him. I asked if someone could come to school tomorrow because I wanted to make a card for him. I also wanted to have the class write him good-bye letters. She said she would try to stop by. I made him a card with inspirational quotes and words of encouragement. The students each wrote him a letter. Here is an excerpt from one of those letters:

> I know you did not mean to get angry at me last week. I know you are sorry and I forgive you. I'm going to miss you. I'm glad you came into our class. I liked being your reading buddy. I will pray to God for you.

Each letter was touching and reminded me how forgiving and understanding children can be. Most of the class knew something was wrong with Steven, but they acted as if everything was going to be all right. Each one of those letters reignited hope and comforted me. His guardian did come and pick up the letters and I can only hope and pray that he received them.

There is rarely a day that goes by that I do not think of Steven and pray for him. I still have his ruler with his name written boldly in black marker on the back that he left behind the day he left me so abruptly. Each time I come across it I'm reminded of him and our short time together. I stop and pray for protection and guidance over his life. I believe it was no coincidence that this physical reminder of him remains with me to this day.

I often think about those four months that he was in my classroom. I think about what God's purpose could have been in allowing our paths to cross. I believe all things happen for a reason, and I wonder if Steven knows how much I cared for him and tried to help him. I question why things had to end the way they did. I find myself thinking about him and how his life will turn out given all the negative things he has experienced. When those thoughts flood my mind, the only comfort I find is in my faith in God and His mysterious ways. I know God is a faithful God and a God of justice. According to The Bible, "…We know that God causes everything to work together for the good of those who love God and are called according to His purpose for them" (Rom. 8:28 NLT). I have to believe that God has a purpose and a plan for Steven and He will work out that plan for good, or else I have no hope.

Looking back on those four months I believe this hurting young soul was used to teach me lessons about faith and hope that I could not learn anywhere else. This young man taught me that no matter how hard I tried and no matter what I did I could not take away his pain or change his situation. I had to rely on my faith in God and believe in His omniscience and His Omni-presence.

Steven taught me that I do not have all the answers and will never know all the answers. I was reminded through this experience that faith believes in what we cannot see. I believe that God is working in him and is working to bring healing and comfort to his hurting and lonely soul. I hold out hope that God is true to His Word and will allow "all things to work together for good" in this boy's life. I have no idea how he is doing. I have not heard from him or his guardian. As a teacher that often happens. Our students become such a huge part of our lives, then they move on, and we wonder how they will turn out. I'm learning daily to have the faith to believe they will turn out just the way God planned. I pray that Steven will discover God's faithfulness and that he will hold onto the hope that God will never leave him nor forsake him.

LESSON LEARNED: I'm learning that faith and hope, just like patience and self-control, are developed through our experiences. God knows everything before it happens. I believe He sees the beginning, middle, and the end of each life all in a glance. If we trust God, He will work everything out for our good no matter how bad things may seem. We may not understand His ways or His timing, but we need to remember to live by faith and not by sight.

PEACEFULNESS

"So humble yourselves before God. Resist the Devil, and he will flee from you. Draw close to God, and God will draw close to you..."

—James 4:7-8 NLT

ATTENTION ALL PASSENGERS: Flight 637 is now boarding through Gate 16. Please have your boarding pass and picture ID available for the gate agent."

I had been waiting to hear those words as I fidgeted in my seat in the Miami International Airport. I was filled with excitement and anticipation over how the next sixteen days were going to impact my life. Within hours I would be transported to the land where modern history began and where history was interrupted when God humbled himself by entering humanity in the form of a man named Jesus Christ to demonstrate His love for all people.

Summer vacation had finally arrived. I had planned and saved for over a year to visit Egypt, Jordan, and the Holy Land in Israel. I love to travel and had looked forward to the experience for a long time. I felt the timing of this trip could not have been more perfect. God knew that this was the time in my life to experience the land I had been reading about in His Word. He also knew I could use a reminder about His faithfulness in all things since I was still unsettled about the events of the past school year.

The trip renewed my faith and reinforced my hope in God's promises. We started in Egypt and followed the path the Jewish people took so many years ago during the Exodus through the desert to Mount Sinai. Early on Father's Day morning I hiked up the holy mountain where the Ten Commandments were given to Moses by God.

As I watched the sunrise, I marveled at its beauty and sat in awe as darkness gave way to light, and the sky changed every different color you could imagine. As one young man from our tour started to play his guitar, others joined him with songs of praise and worship. I stared at the sky and thanked my Heavenly Father for all He had done for me. It was an incredible way to spend Father's Day.

We stopped at what appeared to be a deep well made of stones in the middle of the desert. I learned from our tour guide that this site called *Marah* was the place where God gave Moses the power to turn the bitter well water to sweet well water, so the Jewish people could quench their parched throats (Ex. 15:23 NLT). We travelled to a resting place The Bible calls *Elim*, "where there were twelve springs and seventy palm trees..." (Ex. 15:27 NLT). Sure enough, I saw the twelve springs and seventy palm trees! The Bible was starting to become so real to me.

We boarded a huge catamaran that crossed over the same Red Sea, which God miraculously parted to aid the Jewish slaves in their escape from the Egyptian army thousands of years ago. We finally arrived in the Holy Land after spending some time in Jordan and visiting the hidden city of Petra. I spent ten days walking where Jesus walked and experiencing all that Israel had to offer. We visited the Garden of Gethsemane where Jesus agonized amongst the olive trees about His impending death and immense suffering. I followed the Via Dolorosa ("Way of Suffering"), which was the path Jesus walked, bloody, beaten, and ridiculed the day of His crucifixion. Sorrow filled my heart as I tried to imagine how Jesus felt that awful and dreaded day. My sorrow soon turned into joy upon visiting the Garden Tomb where Jesus' body once laid before

He was resurrected and returned to the heights of heaven. The sign on the entrance to the tomb said it all, "He is risen!" Jesus' presence became such a part of me. The sense of hope and joy I felt is beyond anything I have experienced on any trip before. Israel is an amazing place and I intend to return again soon. After I returned home, I began to see how that trip strengthened my faith. I have felt a calming peacefulness that has remained with me ever since.

That summer and throughout the school year I started attending more teacher training workshops to improve my teaching skills especially in the area of reading. I attended a few new teacher workshops, but really had not made time to do much more than that. I wanted to gain more insight into reading strategies and skills since more and more students seemed to be below level in reading. It was an area I lacked knowledge and I knew the workshops would help me gain valuable insight.

As usual the timing was perfect since I was about to meet a student who would need a tremendous amount of my help and knowledge in the area of reading. As I began to get to know him, I never realized that he was going to provide me with a tremendous revelation as well. He was a very quiet and polite young man who had difficulty with reading comprehension and vocabulary. He tried hard, but struggled with sounding out words and remembering details from a story. He often did not do well on reading tests and assignments and began to fear them. I knew his family well since I taught his older sister my first year. They had spoken to me privately about their Christian faith and the fact that their son loved to watch Christian pastors preaching on television.

His mom would tell me how he would listen to the programs and then recite to her, almost verbatim, the messages that were shared. She had a hard time understanding why he could not remember details in stories he read. I did not have any answers.

As the weeks passed, I worked closely with him in small reading group and one-on-one, implementing some of the reading strategies I learned from the workshops. We would complete phonics activities using vowel and consonant sounds, prefix and suffix flashcards, short comprehension passages and vocabulary activities together. He also used interactive reading software that targeted these areas as well. I did observe some improvement, but his reading tests scores were still very low.

I also noticed that he had a low self-esteem; he was always putting himself down and didn't seem to have any self-confidence. He dreaded reading aloud in class and continued to dread taking reading tests. I would praise him and encourage him, along with his parents, in an attempt to better his self-esteem, but it did not appear to be working.

One day he broke down after another student made fun of him while he was reading aloud. I called him up to my desk, after reprimanding the other student, and tried to calm him down. He just kept sobbing and sobbing. Once he calmed down, I tried reminding him of how well he had been doing in reading this year and how much progress he made. "It takes time, patience, and practice to get better at something," I said. What he said next would put things into perspective.

"Mr. Fiore, you just don't know how hard it is when you keep having these voices in your head telling you that you can't do it and that you are stupid and stuff like that!"

I sat there dumbfounded not knowing what to say. Sorrow and pain filled my heart. Then immediately I felt prompted to tell him about my experience that first time substituting. I told him how I worried all night about walking into the classroom. I told him how fearful I felt when nobody was listening to me and the class was out of control. What I told him next seemed to make all the difference. I shared with him that while I was travelling home from that terrible first day of substituting, negative thoughts in my mind told me that I wasn't good at teaching and that I should never bother trying again. He smiled and wiped his face.

"See you're not the only one who has bad thoughts, but more importantly what are we going to do about them?" I asked. Neither he nor I said anything further, but we both felt better. I made sure that night to call his mom and explain our conversation. She was so touched that I took the time to share it with her. She said that he never shared that with her and that she would definitely talk to him. Days passed and he never mentioned anything more about it to me. I figured his mom spoke with him and everything would be better.

He continued to improve his reading comprehension and phonics skills, but still scored low on reading tests. Our state standardized tests were coming up and I was concerned. I reflected on my renewed sense of God's faithfulness based on my recent experiences and that provided some comfort. He would, however, need to pass the test or he would be retained, and retaining him would severely damage his already low self-esteem. I continued to work closely with him and prayed for guidance and direction.

A few weeks before the state standardized tests, he came up to my desk and asked to talk. He told me that over the last week he had been watching his favorite Christian pastor on television and the pastor spoke about stopping negative thoughts and replacing them with good thoughts. He continued telling me the pastor said one of the ways the Devil tries to harm us and steal our peace is by using negative thoughts. The best way to stop those negative thoughts and experience peace is to pray to God, in Jesus' name, for help. After we stop the negative thoughts we then need to begin thinking good thoughts on purpose. I was astonished at his recollection and description of this lesson he learned. I told him how proud I was of him for listening and remembering all those details. He smiled and then returned to his seat. I continued to think about the power of this simple truth he shared with me. He did end up passing the state standardized test in reading and continued to do much better that year. I knew he would still need to work hard on his reading and his self-confidence, but that revelation would prove to be very valuable to him on his journey through life. I know it was to me.

Every time I think or share that story with someone I get chills. It still amazes me how Jesus spoke to his heart through that pastor's message and gave him a revelation that will change his life forever. He was open and available to hear the truth and that is exactly what he received. I'm touched God placed me there at that moment to reinforce His message. Words are powerful but as I have learned over the years thoughts are even more powerful. I have learned to memorize and recite Bible verses like the one listed at the beginning of this chapter, to help give me peace and strength during the times I feel negative thoughts creeping into my mind.

I have to confess I still struggle with negative thinking at times, but I'm getting better at recognizing the pattern and changing it. I'm trying to replace bad thoughts with good thoughts and rely on Jesus' strength for help, but it is not always so easy. I believe this student and his story helped teach me a valuable lesson about my thought life and about finding true peace. I will never forget him or the lesson.

He often talked about becoming a pastor when he grew up. I told him and his parents that I thought he would make an awesome pastor one day. I believe the peace he discovered by learning how to deal with his negative thoughts will guide his heart and mind as he journeys through life.

It never ceases to amaze me how some students who seem so quiet and shy really have so much to share. As a teacher I need to remember to listen more often because I never know when God might be willing to speak through one of His children. After all, He chose to speak to us about the meaning of true love through the life and sacrifice of His one and only son Jesus. This experience has reminded me that God is the source of true peacefulness in this negative world. We need to keep our thoughts and mind focused on Him.

> LESSON LEARNED: Thousands of thoughts run through our minds each day. Thoughts are powerful and can have either a positive or negative result on our life. As I have learned, with Jesus' help, we can choose to resist negative thoughts and replace them with positive thoughts. As I purposely practice this daily, I'm growing to experience true peace which can only be found through knowing God's promises.

A Joyful Spirit

"For we are God's masterpiece. He has created us anew in Christ Jesus, so that we can do the good things He planned for us long ago."

—Eph. 2:10 NLT

Michael was diagnosed at birth with cerebral palsy. He was in a wheelchair and most of the muscles in his body were affected. He did not have mobility in his legs; he had limited mobility and control of his arms; he could not write and needed a teacher's aide to assist him daily. He had difficulty speaking and reading since his diaphragm muscles were also affected by the disability.

Michael was just finishing second grade and would soon be a third grader. He was talking in the hallway outside my classroom door about his plans for the summer and the fact that he could not wait to be in third grade, while smiling and laughing with his brother.

His mother introduced herself to me and asked if she could talk with me. She asked if I would be willing to be her son's teacher next year. I was honored, but also fearful. I had never taught a child with cerebral palsy before and wasn't sure I would be the best fit for him. I told his mother we would need to check with the administration and thanked her very much for thinking of me.

Summer vacation began and I started to worry about what to do. I prayed for direction, as I have done countless times before, and asked that if it was God's will that He give me the wisdom and confidence to handle this assignment. I chose to trust Him and to try not to worry. My prayer was answered the first week of August when we received our class lists for the new school year and Michael's name was on it. I called each student's family and invited them to our third grade orientation. The first call I made was to his mother. I will never forget our conversation. We spoke for what seemed like hours, and I shared my concerns and fears about teaching her son. I told her that I did not have the experience I needed but I was willing to do my best. Of course, she pledged her and her husband's support, which would prove to be invaluable as the school year began. I was also blessed with a teacher's aide who knew the family well and had worked with them for the last three years. She proved to be like God's invisible hand placed into my life to walk me through the uncertainty that lie ahead. I was still concerned about my lack of experience, but I made a decision to stop agonizing over it.

As I started to learn about Michael and his skills and strengths, I began to feel a bit more at ease. I noticed the other students in the class did as well. I began discovering more and more of what he could do and tried to focus less on the things he could not do, which certainly required adjusting the way I taught and planned my lessons. I knew my previous lessons on patience would be tested once again, and I had to learn how to be more flexible. This was not a characteristic that came easy to a Type-A personality like me. I liked to stick to my schedule and would become frustrated when things did not always go as planned.

There were many days when I had to rework my lesson plans. I had to learn to think more carefully about how to present material that would meet his needs, remembering he could not write without assistance. I had to be sensitive to the way I arranged my classroom to accommodate for his wheelchair. I had to budget extra time when transitioning from subject to subject and from lunch to specials classes. I also worked closely with his aide to modify assignments to ensure he could complete them along with the rest of the class. On a daily basis, I was reminded to be flexible, patient and willing to adapt to whatever challenges arose.

Michael always had an infectious smile on his face. On days when I would come to school feeling a bit down or frustrated over something small, he would enter the room and my mood immediately changed. He had that effect on many other people too, especially his fellow students.

As the year went on, I discovered that Michael was definitely a creative genius. He especially enjoyed writing, and would think up amazing stories with depth and meaning, then dictate his thoughts and ideas to his aide. He never lacked a writing partner. The other students always wanted to work with him and enjoyed watching him create masterpieces. They often would offer to be his "secretary" and write for him as he shared his ideas. I would watch in awe as my students learned an important lesson on the value of feeling needed. I could not have orchestrated a better way to instill in them the importance of this basic human desire.

One of Michael's favorite writing activities was to create his own comic strips in our writing center. I looked forward to reading all of his work and was amazed at the way he implemented the writing strategies he learned in class. He was like a sponge and soaked up every detail he could about the writing process. He did the same in math, remembering each lesson with almost perfect clarity. He sometimes struggled with the execution of the concept, but he never gave up. His aide and I worked with him one-on-one each week and he began to gain more confidence in his math skills. He would often tell me that math was not his favorite subject, but he refused to let that stop him from mastering it. He would sometimes become frustrated and feel like giving up, but down deep he was determined. He would often say, "I want, I w-a-n-t to get it like everyone e-l-s-e!" I believe that was the driving force that motivated him in many other things as well. He wanted to be like all the other students and in my eyes he was like them in more ways than he realized. I would always tell him, "You can do it if you put your mind to it!"

Michael's spirit was unyielding; he did whatever he had to do to make sure he was not behind. His mother would often tell me he would not rest until he finished his math homework, even if it took hours! She was constantly at his side encouraging and supporting him in every way. I observed his influence on the other students. He set such a high expectation for himself that he naturally motivated the other students to do the same. I could not have crafted a better method of motivation myself.

One of my fondest memories of Michael was his role as "mayor." We were working on a social studies unit about communities, which I was going to videotape for my National Board of Professional Teaching Standards (NBPTS) certification, the highest level of certification available for teachers in the United States. It involves many different components such as successfully demonstrating classroom learning strategies (both through writing and videotape) and by taking a computer-based test of teaching knowledge. The students knew it was important for me, so they followed directions and did their best since I needed to submit this as part of the process to obtain my certification.

I split the students into teams of five and each team had to create their own "Community in a Box." They were given an empty cardboard box and had to create a community including people, buildings and streets. Then they needed to decorate the outside of the box with an item that represented their own heritage to demonstrate the diversity between the team members. Michael immediately took charge of his team as captain and made sure everyone was assigned a task as I had requested. They named their new community "New City." Once the community was built they needed to create laws for their new community and select a mayor. He was unanimously elected mayor of New City by the "citizens."

Michael practiced his role day after day, wanting it to be perfect. He often struggled when it came to speaking for long periods of time due to his lack of control over his diaphragm muscles. We reminded him to take deep breaths and relax.

The day of the taping arrived and Michael came dressed in a suit and tie ready to begin the town meeting. His mom told me he could barely sleep he was so excited. He began the meeting with his secretary (our teacher's aide) at his side. "Attention, Attention! I call, I call this meeting to order. I'm your m-a-y-o-r. We need to d-e-v-e-l-o-p laws for our city." He did an amazing job delivering his speech and working with the citizens to develop the laws. He took command of the meeting and his ability to lead others was evident. I was so proud of him. Once again, he showed me and the other students that he was capable of doing whatever they could do.

The amount of enthusiasm and dedication Michael displayed helped to remind me that this was not just a class project for him, but a passion. A passion to prove he could do whatever he put his mind to if given the opportunity. Needless to say,

I believe he was one of the reasons I was able to successfully achieve my National Board Certification that year. He challenged me to make sure all my lessons met each of my students' individual needs and that each one felt motivated to learn.

As I looked back on that year, I saw how this special young boy taught me in so many ways. He helped me overcome my fear of not having enough experience and taught me to have more self-confidence in my ability to do things I have never done before. He helped me learn to be more flexible and to be more sensitive to the individual needs of each of my students. He challenged me to find creative ways to teach each lesson so that he could equally participate like all the other students. He reminded me, through his spirit and determination, that God provides each of us with what we need to accomplish the assignment He has given us, whether we realize it or not. He taught me that a child with special needs just wants to be like everyone else. He forced me to look beyond the physical to what lies within each of my students. The body we inhabit is just one piece of who we are; the spirit is the larger force at work within us and it guides the desires of our hearts. Michael proved to me how easy it can be to make the best of any situation if you keep a joyful spirit. He did not let his external circumstances dampen the joy he possessed internally.

Here is an excerpt from the letter I wrote to his parents the last week of school:

He truly believes he can do anything and that faith is what will make all his dreams a reality. I know God will continue to use him during his journey here on earth to teach others lessons about determination, hope and being joyful in all things like only he can...

LESSON LEARNED: God doesn't make mistakes. Each of us is His masterpiece. God created us so we could live out the good plans He has prepared for us. It is up to each of us to accept His plan for our life, make the decision to follow our spirit joyfully, and be determined to never give up no matter how difficult it may seem.

GENTLENESS

"You should be known for the beauty that comes from within, the unfading beauty of a gentle and quiet spirit, which is so precious to God."

—1 Pet. 3:4 NLT

Writing starts from within us and has the ability to evoke feelings in others. What we say can be meaningful but how we say it can be more powerful. Words delivered in a right voice at the right time can make all the difference. I have learned ways to convey that idea to my students when I'm teaching writing. I often share with them many forms of writing by various authors to help them understand this concept. I also try to help them realize how important it is to use their own experiences when they write to make their writing more impactful.

Often times, they lack details in their writing. "Details, details, details are the key," I often say. I use the following activity to convey this point to them. I tell my class that I'm thinking of a student with brown hair; can you guess who it is? (Usually there are several students with brown hair.) They may guess but it is difficult. I then say that the student I'm thinking of has brown hair and is a boy. It still is difficult for them to figure out who it is at this point. Then I say the student is a brown-haired boy wearing glasses with black frames. At this point they usually guess correctly. It is a very simple activity and the parameters can be changed, but it conveys to them the importance of using details to help the reader understand and relate to their writing.

Graphic organizers are another idea I have used to help plan details for my students writing and to get them started. These help them to visually plan out their thought process. I have collected several over the years from other teachers such as drawing a picture of a big umbrella with a long handle on a piece of paper. The student writes his or her topic inside the umbrella. On the handle of the umbrella, the student draws lines and lists the details they want to discuss in his or her writing. It is a great visual and helps the student with mapping out his or her ideas and details before they begin writing.

Some of the best graphic organizers I have seen were the ones created by my students. Each year, after modeling how to use graphic organizers, I give them the assignment of creating their own. I encourage them to be creative and to develop graphic organizers that interest them and ones they will actually use. One of my students who loved to play baseball created an organizer with a baseball bat and balls. On the bat he wrote his topic and on the balls his details for his story. Another student loved ice cream so she drew an ice cream cone with scoops of ice cream. On the ice cream cone she wrote her topic and then on each scoop of ice cream she wrote one detail for her story. She told me it really helped her and made writing more fun. Another student drew a cloud with rain drops. In the cloud, he wrote the topic and on the raindrops his details. Many of the students have found that the graphic organizers help them get their ideas on paper and give them some direction before they start writing their rough draft.

During my fourth year of teaching, there was one particular student who took these writing lessons to heart. I gave the students the assignment of writing a short narrative paragraph. Their objective was to share their personal experience using great details, and the topic was: Think about your best friend and write about an experience with him or her. Here is an excerpt of what I received from this insightful young girl:

> *Oh, hi. Since you're here, I'll tell you about my special friend. My special friend is Jesus. I pray to him and worship him. I know I can always count on him. Here is how we met. My mom, brother, and I were driving to my dad's work when I was young. On the highway we saw rocks. Screeeeetch…we spun out of control. Off to the left, then right, then left, then right, then left again. My mom shouted, "Jesus!, Jesus!, Jesus!" On the left of me a man dressed all in white was walking through cars. I asked my mom who was that man and she said, "He is a miracle, Our Father, He is Jesus!"*

I was stunned. I had known her family well since I had taught her older brother two years ago. They were a wonderful Christian family who made sure to instill faith in Jesus with their children. I learned her name, Ariana, meant "very holy one." Her faith and ability to convey her experiences in such a bold and honest way inspired me. I encouraged her and reminded her to "live what she was learning."

She had a tendency to be a bit bossy and domineering; it was part of her personality. On several occasions she would come to me in tears because some of the other girls did not want to be around her. She kept telling them what to do in a demanding tone and would not listen to what they had to say. I had to remind her that she could not always do the talking and that she needed to treat others the way she wanted to be treated. She replied, "I know, I know, but it is so hard sometimes." Silently I agreed with her. As the teacher I like being in charge of my class and I love to talk, but I also needed to remember to listen to my students. There have also been times I have been quick to reprimand my students using a forceful voice when the message could have been conveyed just as effectively using a gentler tone. Each time I had one of those conversations with her, I felt like God was sending me the same message: "Use your gift of being a bold communicator, but in a gentle and productive way."

Memorial Day was approaching and the school year was coming to a close. The students were working on writing letters and songs in honor of all those soldiers who have lost their lives defending freedom in our country. We had just finished a lesson about how to use voice to make writing more powerful. This time their goal was to use the proper voice when writing. Here is the song she wrote:

> I thank you, I really do. You don't try to hurt us,
> you protect us and I pray that there will be love
> in the world.
> Love not war, Love not war.

I also pray that there will be peace in the world.
Lovely peace, Lovely peace.
The soldiers that die for us rise to the sky to heaven
above the earth. We have to show we care and
we won't forget.
You have to believe so thank you for saving me.
Thank you for saving us and saving our country.
I believe we are free from fighting. I believe!

I was moved beyond words when I read this beautiful song. It was written with such gentleness, which so appropriately complemented her message. She sang it for the class during our talent show. As she sang she delivered the words with such passion. I could not help but think of Jesus when she sang these particular words, "You don't try to hurt us, you protect us and I pray that there will be love in the world. You have to believe so thank you for saving me. Thank you for saving us."

The Christian faith is rooted in that very truth: we all need a Savior since God's standard is perfect and we all have fallen short of His standard through sin. Jesus demonstrated true love by suffering on a cross, dying to save all humanity from the punishment of sin, then rising back to the heights of heaven so each of us could have a right relationship with God. I don't know if that was her intention when writing those verses but it was what I felt in my heart. I was proud of her for writing with such depth and for using such detail. She reminded me that writing can have a powerful effect on people. It can speak to one's heart and evoke strong feelings and beliefs. She spoke out of the gentleness of her heart and it was visible in the beauty of her words.

I learned that sometimes a message delivered with gentleness, like her song can be just as powerful as one delivered with boldness like the narrative she wrote. As a communicator, I need to be more aware of how best to convey my messages to my students. Ariana demonstrated that truth to me. Whether the message is simple or complicated its effectiveness depends on the way it is delivered. In God's infinite wisdom, He speaks to us boldly and gently through His Word. Listening to Him has made all the difference in my life.

> LESSON LEARNED: Our words can be meaningful, but how they are delivered is often what is memorable. As a communicator, I need to be more aware of how my message is being delivered. I'm learning that sometimes boldness may be needed, but words spoken from a gentle and sincere spirit are precious to God.

KINDNESS

"...be kind to each other, tenderhearted, forgiving one and other, just as God through Christ has forgiven you."

—Eph. 4:32 NLT

Kindness as defined by the Oxford dictionary is "the quality of being friendly, generous, and considerate." Each friendly, generous, and considerate act I have experienced has reminded me just how kind the heart of a child can be. Each experience has also helped clarify for me exactly how kindness can change attitudes, emotions and hearts. There have been countless students who have demonstrated the building blocks of kindness. Like most teachers, I have many memorable situations that have touched my heart and that have left lasting impressions on me.

K-indhearted

Children remind me daily what it means to have a heart that is the core to true kindness. My classroom system of rewarding Behavior Bucks for good behavior and for the successful completion of various assignments and tasks allows students to pick a prize from the prize can once they reach their pre-determined goal. One Friday, a girl who had been trying for weeks to earn a chance to pick a prize finally succeeded. She skipped to the prize can and we all cheered as she picked her prize. The smile on her face was even more meaningful for me since I knew she came from a lower income home and did not have many toys of her own. As she turned to walk back to her desk, she noticed the sadness in the eyes of another boy who also had not yet picked a prize. He had been trying hard each week also. Without hesitation, she walked over to him and placed the toy on his desk and smiled. Her kind heart helped to remind me that when we see someone in need and we have the ability to meet that need why not do it? This is a simple but powerful example to me of what being kindhearted is all about.

I-mpact

As a teacher it is sometimes difficult to know just how much of an impact you have had on a child. They are with you for ten months or so, then they move on. You rarely ever see or hear from many of them again. It always touches my heart when a student I taught comes to visit me. Just the fact that he or she took the time to think of me confirms that I did have some kind of an impact on his or her life. Those acts of kindness keep me going and often seem to happen just at the right moments in my life.

One day in particular I was feeling down and questioning my effectiveness as a teacher when I received a knock on my classroom door. It was a student I taught three years prior. He told me he just wanted to stop in to say "Hi." He said he wanted to thank me for helping him with reading because now he is getting mostly As and Bs in middle school. The visit lasted no more than a few minutes, but the memory remains with me. In this busy and hectic world, we often forget how much of an impact a simple thank you can have on someone's state of mind. In my opinion, it is so powerful because it is so personal.

N-otes

I have a folder in my desk at school that I refer to often. It is not like most of my folders that contain lesson plans, district memos, graded papers, or papers to be copied. It is a brightly colored folder full of notes, cards, and letters I have received over the years from students. I call it my "Feel God Folder." I got the idea from a teacher friend of mine. It is a simple idea, but one that has provided me with much joy. I enjoy reading and re-reading the notes, cards, and letters from students on days when I feel discouraged; I always feel better after reading them. Their expressions of kindness remind me that words can change someone's feelings, attitudes, and heart instantly. I don't know many other positions that provide you with this amazing opportunity to receive immediate gratification in such a positive and powerful way.

D-onations

Each year our school sponsors various collection drives for needy families in our community. Most collections are for food. One particular year, we were collecting items for a charity that helped abused and homeless children. We asked the students to donate toys and clothes specifically.

As the days passed, more and more toys and clothes arrived in my classroom. One student brought a brand new teddy bear she had just gotten for her birthday. She told me, "I will miss him, but I know the other kids need him more than me." It touched me to see so many students giving out of the sincerity of their hearts even though many of them were going to miss their toys.

With my car packed I drove the donations to the charity. While driving I remember thinking how much of a difference this delivery would have on the lives of these needy children. We have plenty of opportunities to be a blessing to others if we are willing to allow kindness to drive our desires, like the time my class wanted to donate some of their Behavior Bucks each week to benefit someone else.

As a class we sponsored a child through World Vision, a Christian-based charity. It offers an opportunity to meet the needs of a child somewhere in the world by sending a monthly donation and communicating through letters and cards to encourage the families of the children. Understanding the importance of giving rather than receiving, I sent a letter home to their parents proposing this project. I then told the class that if they donated a certain amount of their Behavior Bucks each month to our needy child, Bernard, I would match their donation with real money and send it to his family. I then said nothing more about it. I placed Bernard's photo and his biography on the bulletin board and what happened those next few weeks amazed me.

Without me prompting or asking any of them, they would donate a few of their Behavior Bucks each month. One student donated all hers for two weeks in a row; she wanted to make sure Bernard would be able to have food. "We have so much food and clothes in our country and I wanted to make sure he could have some," she said.

N-ice

I would be remiss if I did not include examples of the importance of being nice in the process. My students have demonstrated this fact to me over and over throughout the years. As teachers, we sometimes need to remind students of the biblically-based truth to "treat people the way you want to be treated." Once they grasp the concept, they prove it can be simple to do. Holding the door open for someone else or stopping in the hall so an adult could pass through our line without having to wait for our whole class to pass. Saying "thank you" to the cafeteria staff for preparing their lunch. Offering a pencil to a student who does not have one or sharing their snacks with students who forgot theirs. Defending another student who was accused of something he or she did not do. Helping someone pick up something he or she dropped or volunteering to help around the classroom. There are countless more ways my students have shown me how easy it is just to be nice. Our world would be a much kinder place if we all practiced this lesson more often.

E-ncouragement

Everyone needs a source of positive support in their life to overcome areas where they struggle. Encouragement is a form of kindness that provides hope to those who need it. I try each and every day to encourage my students academically, socially, and emotionally. I enjoy it immensely when they encourage me especially when it comes to my creative abilities.

As I mentioned earlier, my students have inspired me to be creative in many areas of my teaching. They have given me ideas I have used to advance my teaching methods. My students never cease to amaze me with their artistic skills. I was never very talented at art and always had a hard time drawing and designing pictures. I guess that is why I appreciate this trait so much in my students.

Over the years, like many teachers, I have received so many beautiful drawings and pictures from my students. Each one conveys to me a different message. I remember one drawing that featured me with a big smile on my face teaching my class. It encouraged me since I believe that is how that student saw me. I have received many other pictures featuring hearts, rainbows, and butterflies, along with kind words. I always feel encouraged especially since many of these images represent hope. I often hang them on my bulletin board for a few weeks to serve as a reminder to me of how those students felt about me. I know parents must feel the same way when they receive such expressions of kindness from their kids. We all need to be encouraged and children seem to know just how to do it in a way that is all their own.

S-miles

A smile is the ultimate non-verbal expression of kindness. Children remind me of this truth every day. A smile when I compliment them on their reading or when they sound out a word and get it correct. A smile when they grasp a math concept they have been struggling with. A smile when they get a great grade on a test. A smile when I hold up their projects and give them praise in front of the class. A smile when they receive compliments about their behavior. I do my best to return the favor and smile at them when they make me proud, which happens every day. Never underestimate the power of a smile and how it can serve as an instant source of joy. Try smiling for no reason at all and see what happens!

S-elflessness

One of the most challenging obstacles to showing kindness, in my opinion, is selfishness. In our world where everything screams, "*It's all about me*" it is sometimes difficult to allow self*less*ness to flow. I need continual reminders to "get myself off my mind." My students have been a big part of my learning experience in this area.

As teachers, we can easily get trapped in the "it's all about me" way of thinking. After all we are in charge of the class and the students need to listen to us. We plan the lessons, we teach the lessons, and we are in control of our classroom. I believe that is true to an extent.

However, I know that things arise that are out of my control and I'm forced to change my way of thinking. This has happened to me many times when teaching lessons, especially in math. I think I know the best way to teach a concept and then it doesn't work and the students don't grasp it. Out of selfishness I would think, *I tried my best and it's not my fault they can't get it*. But selflessness would say I need to change my approach and determine another way to teach this concept and involve the students in that approach.

Another way I have struggled with selfishness is when dealing with some of my students' parents. I sometimes find myself unwilling to accept their suggestion or criticism of my teaching practices. Again, I'm forced to evaluate the situation. Selflessness would take their suggestions into consideration and not take it personally. That is often not easy to do. I have learned on many occasions that I'm not always right just because I'm the teacher. Those times have humbled me and helped me to understand the reason why selflessness is so important in demonstrating kindness when dealing with others.

In our fast paced world we're so easily consumed with our own lives that we often miss the opportunity to focus on someone else. I know when I'm busy and pressed for time, either in the classroom or in my personal life, selfishness flourishes. I need to get my agenda accomplished and I often miss opportunities to demonstrate kindness. I pray daily for a selfless attitude, which can be challenging; but as experiences continue to unfold in my life, especially in my classroom, I'm slowly learning how to take my eyes off myself and place them on others.

LESSON LEARNED: The Bible commands us to be kind, tender-hearted, and forgiving just as God has forgiven us through Jesus. There are many ways to demonstrate kindness towards others on a daily basis. I have learned the challenge is to keep the focus off ourselves so we can be open to opportunities to meet the needs of others. As I practice this truth, God continues to fulfill all my needs.

LOVE

"Love is patient and kind. Love is not jealous or boastful or proud or rude. Love does not demand its own way. Love is not irritable, and it keeps no record of when it has been wronged. It is never glad about injustice but rejoices whenever the truth wins out. Love never gives up, never loses faith, is always hopeful, and endures through every circumstance."

—1 Cor. 13:4-7 NLT

LOVE YOU and I'm proud of you!
Have a great day!
Love, Mom.

I noticed this message written on a yellow sticky note in the homework binder of one of my students.

Eric was a blonde and energetic boy. He loved to talk and express his feelings. He reminded me so much of myself in third grade, minus the blonde hair. As I grew close to his family I began to realize how much they reminded me of my own family. Love was their foundation.

I was fortunate enough to have taught both Eric and his sister over the years. Their mom volunteered daily with the PTA and was involved in all aspects of their lives. She dropped them off at school and greeted them every day with a hug and a, "How was your day?" Notes always seemed to appear on days when we were having a test or an oral presentation was due. It is amazing how a simple note can change the course of a child's day. She made sure she always knew how they were doing both academically and socially. She made it a priority to stay involved and connected in their school day.

Eric's dad was in the medical profession and travelled often, but always managed to make sure he was there for conferences and important school functions. I will never forget the time he was over-seas at a medical conference and flew over twelve hours just to attend our school's PTA carnival, only to turn around and fly twelve hours back. He knew how important it was to his kids and his wife since she was the chairperson for the carnival. He made the time to be there. The look on his son's face was priceless when he surprised him that October day. Eric's facial expression has forever reminded me that there is no substitute for a parent's love, time, and attention. Sometimes true love requires sacrifice. I have learned to develop a deeper appreciation for my family and the love I received as a child thanks to experiences like this one.

My younger brother and I grew up in a Christian home with parents who demonstrated love on a daily basis. My mom operated her own nursery school out of our house when we were growing up so she could always be there for us. She was always ready and waiting to hear all about our day regardless of what kind of day she had. She would often sit patiently and work on homework with us for hours. She gave so unselfishly of her time. She was always involved in our school life and never missed a parent conference, soccer game, or school play.

My dad worked long hours for a construction company, but managed to find time to coach our little league games and take us to work with him on Saturdays. We always had dinner together. That was our time to share the events of our day with each other. No matter how tight money was, my parents found the resources to take us on many weekend camping trips and annual summer vacations. My parents instilled in me what it means to be a true family. I'm forever grateful to both of them for all the sacrifices they made in order to demonstrate their love for my brother and me.

When I became a teacher and started interacting with all kinds of families I began to realize how truly blessed I was as a child. It seems like families have gotten a lot more complicated since I was growing up. These days there are so many broken families and children are facing so many emotional issues. Families are also busy. Schedules are involved and there never seems to be enough time in the day. A parent's job is not an easy one and I have come to appreciate that more and more over the years.

I know not everyone was as fortunate as me to grow up in such a loving and caring home with both a mom and a dad. There are many parents who did not have good role models growing up and were not shown love. In turn they may have a difficult time showing love to their children or understanding what love is all about.

I have learned from my students that what they seem to want most of all besides their parent's love is their time and attention. I'm so grateful that I had both growing up; some things don't change. Nothing can take the place of a parent attending his or her child's play or game. Nothing can take the place of a parent asking about his or her day at school or about his or her friends. Nothing can take the place of a parent's hug or words of encouragement. Nothing can replace a parent making the time to spend with his or her child. These are all simple but powerful expressions of love parents can do regardless of their background, if they make it a priority. Love is about giving of yourself, and children so desperately want to receive it and feel it.

As I read the Bible verse on love in the beginning of this chapter over and over I began to think about my years as a teacher. It started to become more apparent to me how God has weaved lessons on love through so many of my experiences. Isn't that the way it is in life? Once you look back and put together the pieces the whole picture begins to emerge just like with a puzzle! I began to discover that love is not just an emotion we feel around the people we love, but it is also a decision we make daily.

Love is patient and kind. Pedro, my student who did not speak any English, along with the boy who challenged my teaching abilities through his lack of effort and apathetic behavior, helped to show me that I needed to be more patient. Countless other students over the years have also reminded me of just how much I need to practice patience. I do not think a day has gone by since I began teaching that a student or a class has not reminded me of this truth.

I believe God has been using my students all along to challenge me to see that a big component of true love is being patient. I believe they have reminded me that love also is concerned with being kind and it acts out of pure intention. It can be expressed by selflessness and thinking of others above yourself, just like the young girl did when she gave away the toy she worked so hard to earn from our class prize can. My students have demonstrated that love can be expressed by writing kind notes and drawing pictures that provide encouragement or by stopping by for a personal visit. Kindness can be displayed by just being nice and practicing "The Golden Rule." It can be easily shown through a smile that can instantly change a person's attitude. Being patient and kind is often a decision. We need to purposefully decide to act that way regardless of how we feel. I have realized that when we make the decision to be patient and kind on a daily basis a loving response manifests itself. My students have reinforced the truth of this very important equation: PATIENCE + KINDNESS = LOVE.

Love is not jealous or boastful or proud or rude. Love does not demand its own way. It has become easier for me to see that love is not boastful or proud. My students have shown me countless ways to become more creative in my teaching. Iolani, one of my most creative students, introduced me to the concept of "Class Court" while another one helped me learn to keep my students more engaged using the "Slam Dunk" idea. It humbles me to admit these ideas and many others were not my own. It reminds me to not get too proud of my own efforts.

Students like Michael have forced me to realize there is always a lesson I will need to learn. Just when I was feeling confident and proud of my teaching strategies, I needed to change and adapt to accommodate his special needs due to his cerebral palsy. He also reminded me, along with his class, that God placed them there that year to help me earn my National Board Certification. It was not all my work, but their work that made it possible too. I was reminded of this equation: LOVE $\neq$ PRIDE.

I discovered how another one of my students taught me that love cannot boast. He helped me learn a successful strategy for dealing with negative thinking. He taught me to replace negative thoughts by praying for strength to overcome them and by replacing them with God's thoughts. To think an eight-year-old boy helped me conquer something I had been dealing with since I was a boy myself; that was no accident. I certainly cannot boast that this revelation happened because of anything I did.

Over the years my students have shown me that love doesn't demand its own way. As a teacher, I plan the lessons, I teach the lessons, and control the classroom to an extent. However, I know that when things arise that are out of my control, I'm forced to take a different approach and change my way of thinking. This has happened many times when teaching lessons, especially in math. I think I know the best way to teach a concept and then it doesn't work and the students don't grasp it.

I remember a lesson I was teaching on rounding numbers. Most of the students did not understand it even after I tried several different approaches. I spoke with several other teachers and one of them suggested I incorporate music into the lesson. I used the rhyme "4 or less, let it rest and 5 or more, let it soar" to help the students decide when to round the identified number up or down. It helped immensely and by using music the students retained the strategy. I was forced to change what I thought was the most effective method. This has also happened when giving directions for class projects. So many times I feel I have been thorough in explaining the directions of a project, yet confusion ensues. I can get upset and blame them or I can decide to explain the directions again using a different strategy.

Love requires a decision.

We need to decide not to be selfish by demanding our own way which demonstrates our true capacity to love.

Love is not irritable, and it keeps no record of when it has been wronged. I'm still learning this lesson on love and I assume I will be for a long time. It is hard not get irritated when you have to repeat yourself over and over or when students don't follow directions. I have learned this lesson continually when I encounter students who have Attention Deficit Disorder (ADD) or Attention Deficit Hyperactivity Disorder (ADHD). I often get so upset when they do not stay focused. I have to constantly stand by their side to keep them on task. I sometimes have to stop instruction to redirect them back to our lesson several times a day. These students quickly remind me of how God must feel when it takes me multiple times to listen and obey His Word or the lessons He is trying to teach me during the course of a day.

When I lose my patience with these students I'm reminded that God keeps no record of our wrongs or the times when we fail if we trust in Jesus for forgiveness. I need to make the decision to be quick to forgive and not hold it against them. We are all humans and will make mistakes. I need to practice making the decision each day not to get irritated when students don't follow my directions. That is certainly not easy to do, but that is what the Bible states is an essential ingredient for love. I need to continually remember: LOVE = FORGIVENESS.

Love never gives up, never loses faith, is always hopeful, and endures through every circumstance. As

Jesus said, "…Let the children come to me. Don't stop them! For the Kingdom of God belongs to such as these" (Mark 10:14 NLT). We need to come to God with the faith of a child. Children by nature are very positive and hopeful. I believe I am surrounded each day with hope that is displayed through my students. These eight- and nine-year-olds have their entire life ahead of them and they can do or be anything they desire if they have faith and believe in themselves.

Each one of my students writes goals for themselves the first few weeks of school. They refer to those goals throughout the year and we celebrate when they achieve them. If they don't, I encourage them to try again. Toward the end of the school year we also talk about what they want to do when they grow up. The answers usually range from model to millionaire. Their hope is evident. They believe it is possible.

This hope has encouraged me when I sometimes get discouraged. I'm also encouraged and hopeful when I receive an email, note, or personal visit from a student after he or she has left my class. It is so rewarding to know he or she hasn't forgotten me and that maybe I did make a difference in his or her life in some way.

The Bible states loves never gives up. I have to believe that is true or else I would hold out no hope for Stephen's future, the boy who was abused and withdrawn from my class, and returned to the foster care system. His circumstances might easily cause him to give up on himself. I believe God taught me through Stephen that no matter how bad things look there is always hope. Stephen may not see it and I may not see it, but it is there. I was reminded through his experience that faith believes in what we cannot see. I believe that God is working in him and is working to bring healing and comfort to his hurting and lonely soul. I have not seen or heard from Stephen, but I believe in my heart there is hope for his future. Love promises to endure through every circumstance.

Over the years there have been other students, similar to Stephen, who have caused me to question this promise. I sometimes wonder how they will make it. If I truly believe the Bible then I must believe in God's promises because love is always hopeful. Hope and faith are love decisions we make. We have to purposely decide to stay hopeful and faithful even when our circumstances make us feel differently. If we make the right decision then we can make it through any circumstance since love promises to endure through it all. It can be summarized this way: LOVE – FAITH $\neq$ HOPE.

What we do with the time we are given each day often reveals our true priorities in life. I have learned from children that they don't necessarily look at how many minutes we spend with them, but rather what moments comprise our time with them. Moments make memories in their minds that remind them what it feels like to be loved and cared for. I'm so grateful for all the happy childhood memories that have helped make me who I am today and for feeling love from the moment I was born. My students have made me appreciate that more than ever before in my life. I'm thankful for the experiences with my students and their families which have made me appreciate that love can endure through all circumstances. It's reassuring to know love never gives up and always has hope. Love is always a worthwhile investment. It is the only virtue that will last forever.

LESSON LEARNED: Love is all around us. I have learned that love is not just an emotion, but a decision. We can choose through our experiences and God's help to be patient and kind instead of proud and boastful. We can choose to not get irritated and to never give up and always remain hopeful. God is our Father, the Ultimate Parent, and we all are His children. What better role model could we ask for? He is kind, patient, slow to anger, and full of unending love. He takes the time each day to show us His love, all we need to do is believe it and receive it. "…God so loved the world that He gave His only Son, so that everyone who believes in Him will not perish but have eternal life" (John 3:16 NLT).

Lesson 10

THE SPIRITUAL PUZZLE

"But when the Holy Spirit controls our lives, He will produce this kind of fruit in us: love, joy, peace, patience, kindness, goodness, faithfulness, gentleness and self-control..."

—Gal. 5:22-23 NLT

Looking back on those first memories as a substitute teacher through the present, I would never have imagined that God would use my students and experiences in the classroom to provide such insight into my life and to bring me into a closer relationship with Himself through Jesus. I'm so grateful for the purpose each one of them has played and will play in my life.

The Bible verse above is the completed picture that each puzzle piece of this book has formed. I always knew love, joy, peace, patience, kindness, goodness, faithfulness, gentleness, and self-control were important virtues in life, but I never knew how much God wanted to help me recognize and develop these virtues in my own life. That very first day as a substitute teacher I learned valuable lessons about overcoming fear, worry, and doubt, which have proven to be obstacles in my life on many occasions. Overcoming them continues with each new student God sends my way to reinforce the lessons previous students have taught me. I'm sure that was why my weaknesses were my earliest roadblocks. God knew I would need to be taught over and over with the help of my students.

My first year of teaching third grade tested my patience and self-control and taught me I still need development in these areas also. My students have challenged me to be creative and to use that childhood gift that God blessed me with. They often remind me that anything is possible when you have child-like faith.

Over the last several years, I have witnessed countless acts of kindness, which has helped me appreciate the gentle heart of a child, and has taught me that being kind is really very simple. I felt love growing up, but often took it for granted. By working with so many different students over the years, I have learned just how fortunate I was to have such loving childhood memories. I know there are many families who are broken and need to experience love, and there are also many other families who are willing to teach them through their example. I have learned that love is a decision we can make each day if we allow God to use the people and experiences in our life to guide us.

What is your purpose in life? I used to think that was another way of asking, " What career path will you take or what goals do you have?" Like many others, I have spent many hours trying to find out the answer to that question over the years. After completing two college degrees, excelling in lucrative jobs in the corporate world, and now teaching, I have slowly come to learn that my purpose is not really about how many degrees I have, which job title I hold or how many personal goals I have accomplished. Thanks to God's goodness, I have come to realize that purpose is much bigger than that.

Purpose is more about surrendering my life to Jesus by following His example and allowing Him to use the people and experiences in my life to make me more of who He wants me to be. All the gifts and talents I have are from Him; I believe more than ever that He should have full control over what I do with those gifts and talents. I pray for His purpose for my life each day. Right now, I believe I'm fulfilling that purpose through teaching. Only God knows what the future holds. Now that I'm slowly learning to take the focus regarding my purpose off myself, I have found the freedom to enjoy my life much more.

God's Holy Spirit works to produce love, joy, peace, patience, kindness, goodness, faithfulness, gentleness, and self-control. I believe we each have seeds of these virtues planted within us. If we allow God to direct our path and purpose through His Holy Spirit, He will nurture those seeds and allow them to take root in our life through our circumstances and experiences.

It has been so rewarding to see how this spiritual puzzle has come together in my life. Once I started to sense the growth of these virtues in my life I began to gain a thirst for more spiritual wisdom within God's Word. Of course, the growing process is never easy and takes time. A small seedling planted in the ground can grow into a beautiful creation over time if given the proper care and much light. Our life is really not that much different.

The Bible has been the light in my life that has made all the difference; it has guided my path through some dark and uncertain times and has served as my beacon of hope. It has led me to a personal relationship with Jesus. My prayer is that more teachers find their true purpose by surrendering their heart, mind, and spirit to The One and Only True God who created everything and knows everyone of their needs just like He knows everyone of mine. It astounds me to think that God knew way back in my childhood days when I was "teaching" my imaginary students that I would one day be learning such life-changing lessons from real ones. That's why I have come to expect God to send me a classroom full of His little messengers each year.

> *"Now glory be to God! By His mighty power at work within us, He is able to accomplish infinitely more than we would ever dare to ask or hope."*
>
> —Eph. 3:20 NLT

Scripture Flashcards

Cut out these Bible quotes from each chapter and make them into flashcards. Memorize them and allow the power of God's Word to help you develop these virtues in your life. Visit www. whattheyhavetaughtme.com for formatted printable versions of each flashcard.

Doubt, Worry and Fear:

"Don't worry about anything; instead, pray about everything. Tell God what you need and thank Him for all He has done. If you do this, you will experience God's peace, which is far more wonderful than the human mind can understand. His peace will guard your hearts and minds as you live in Christ Jesus."

—Philippians 4:6-7 NLT

Patience and Self-Control:

"Knowing God leads to self-control. Self-control leads to patient endurance, and patient endurance leads to godliness."

—2 Peter 1:6 NLT

God's Goodness:

God has given gifts to each of you from His great variety of spiritual gifts. Manage them well so that God's generosity can flow through you."

—1 Peter 4:10 NLT

Faithfulness:

"What is faith? It is the confident assurance that what we hope for is going to happen. It is the evidence of things we cannot yet see."

—Hebrews 11:1 NLT

Peacefulness:

"So humble yourselves before God. Resist the Devil, and he will flee from you. Draw close to God, and God will draw close to you…"
—James 4:7-8 NLT

A Joyful Spirit:

"For we are God's masterpiece. He has created us anew in Christ Jesus, so that we can do the good things He planned for us long ago."
—Ephesians 2:10 NLT

Gentleness:

"You should be known for the beauty that comes from within, the unfading beauty of a gentle and quiet spirit, which is so precious to God."
—1 Peter 3:4 NLT

Kindness:

…be kind to each other, tenderhearted, forgiving one another just as God through Christ has forgiven you."
—Ephesians 4:32 NLT

Love:

"Love is patient and kind. Love is not jealous or boastful or proud or rude. Love does not demand its own way. Love is not irritable, and it keeps no record of when it has been wronged. It is never glad about injustice but rejoices whenever the truth wins out. Love never gives up, never loses faith, is always hopeful, and endures through every circumstance."
—1 Corinthians 13:4-7 NLT

The Spiritual Puzzle:

"But when the Holy Spirit controls our lives, He will produce this kind of fruit in us: love, joy, peace, patience, kindness, goodness, faithfulness, gentleness, and self-control…"
—Galatians 5:22-23 NLT

CPSIA information can be obtained
at www.ICGtesting.com
Printed in the USA
LVHW011554180820
663527LV00005B/548

9 780615 962061